Transport

Elizabeth Nonweiler

raintree

big rig

tandem

rocket

tram

blimp

ox cart

helibus

pedicab

dog sled

catamaran

farm tractor

electric car

13

Interesting facts about the pictures

page 2: A **big rig** is the American name for a large truck with a towing engine at the front and a trailer behind to carry freight. In the UK it is called an articulated lorry.

page 3: A **tandem** bicycle has two or more seats, one behind the other. It is difficult to balance on a tandem at first, but it gets easier with practice. These children are enjoying a ride on a road in Thailand.

page 4: A **rocket** takes off into the sky by driving its exhaust out onto the ground very fast to push it up. This rocket is carrying a spaceship with people in it out of Earth's atmosphere into space to orbit Earth.

page 5: **Trams** run on tracks along the road. The first tram was in Wales and was pulled by horses. Most modern trams use electricity, usually from a wire overhead. Trams usually have a driver cab at both ends.

page 6: A **blimp** is a non-rigid airship. It is filled with a light gas called helium that lifts it up and keeps it in shape. Blimps can stay in the air for days.

page 7: **Ox carts** are carts pulled by oxen. They were often used on farms before tractors were available. This ox cart is being used on a rice field where the ground is so wet a heavy tractor might get stuck.

page 8: A **helibus** is a big helicopter for carrying people. Some helibuses are used for search and rescue. This helibus is for carrying people to work on an oil rig out at sea.

page 9: **Pedicabs** are like taxis for taking people places. Instead of engines they have pedals. This pedicab is on a road in Hanoi, a big city in Vietnam. The canopy shades the passenger from the hot sun.

page 10: **Dog sleds** are sleds pulled by dogs over ice or snow. If the dogs are well looked after, they can pull a sled fast a long way. Once they were used a lot, but now snowmobiles are used more often.

page 11: A **catamaran** has two hulls instead of one, which helps it to move fast. Some catamarans have sails. This one is a ferry for carrying people from Naples, a large city in Italy, to a nearby island.

page 12: A **farm tractor** can pull heavy loads across fields, like machinery for ploughing, planting and harvesting. This one is pulling a tank full of grain. Tractors have big wheels so they can move on soft ground.

page 13: **Electric cars** use electricity instead of petrol to make them go. They are more expensive to buy than other cars, but cheaper to run because electricity costs less than petrol. This car is recharging its batteries.

Letter-sound correspondences

Level 1 books cover the following letter-sound correspondences.
Letter-sound correspondences highlighted in **green** can be found
in this book.

ant	big	cat	dog	egg	fish	get	hot	it
jet	key	let	man	nut	off	pan	queen	run
sun	tap	up	van	wet	box	yes	zoo	

duck	fish	chips	sing	thin this	keep	look moon	art	corn